PROHIBITION

America Makes Alcohol Illegal

BY DANIEL COHEN

Spotlight on American History
The Millbrook Press • Brookfield, Connecticut

Library of Congress Cataloging-in-Publication Data
Cohen, Daniel, 1936–
Prohibition : America makes alcohol illegal / by Daniel Cohen.
    p.   cm.— (Spotlight on American history)
Includes bibliographical references and index.
Summary: Discusses temperance movements in the United States, and
the impact that the prohibition of alcohol had on the nation.
ISBN 1-56294-529-7
1. Prohibition—United States—History—Juvenile literature.
2. Temperance—United States—History—Juvenile literature.
[1. Prohibition. 2. Temperance.] I. Title. II. Series.
HV5089.C663 1995 363.4′1′0973—dc20 94-37756 CIP   AC

Cover photograph courtesy of the National Archives

Photographs courtesy of The Bettmann Archive: pp. 8, 32, 40, 42, 51,
56; Library of Congress: pp. 10, 17, 19, 21, 23, 25, 26–27, 37, 39, 47, 55;
The Museum of the City of New York: pp. 29 ("The Drunkard's Progress:
From the First Glass to the Grave," N. Currier, 1846), 48 (Ben Shahn,
"Federal Agents Pouring Wine Down a Sewer," c. 1934, L1226.3A).

Published by The Millbrook Press
2 Old New Milford Road, Brookfield, Connecticut 06804

Contents

1

THE FUNERAL OF JOHN BARLEYCORN

One minute after midnight on January 16, 1920, it became illegal to buy, sell, manufacture, or transport any alcoholic beverage within the United States and its territories.

There were some limited exceptions. Alcohol could still be sold for medicinal purposes. Sacramental wine would be available for churches and synagogues. Anyone who had a stock of liquor at home could drink it at home, but it couldn't be taken anywhere else. And once the stock was gone that was it—there would be no more.

The Eighteenth Amendment to the Constitution was in effect; the era that was to be known as Prohibition had begun.

Across the nation the event was greeted in a variety of ways.

There was, for example, a last-minute panic. The Eighteenth Amendment had been ratified a year earlier. It was quite simple. Intoxicating beverages were prohibited. People were supposed to

The proposal to forbid the drinking, manufacture, sale, and transportation of alcoholic beverages was not popular in many parts of the United States. This lithograph of the period is entitled, "A cold reception everywhere."

have had time to get used to the idea. The law that spelled out exactly how Prohibition was to be enforced, and what exceptions were allowed—commonly called the Volstead Act—was quite complicated. It wasn't passed until October 28, 1919, less than three months before Prohibition was to go into effect.

A lot of people believed that it would be legal to store private stocks of liquor in commercial warehouses and safe deposit vaults. Those who had the money built up large private hoards. Then, just a day before the start of Prohibition, a federal judge unexpectedly ruled that all liquor that was not actually in a person's home could be seized after January 16.

Throughout the country there was a mad scramble as hoarders stuffed everything from limousines to baby carriages with bottles to get them to the safety of their homes.

As the new "dry" era dawned it was greeted with vastly different moods. In the saloons of many big cities there was a sort of stunned disbelief. Up to the very last minute bartenders and patrons alike simply refused to believe that Prohibition would be enforced. Liquor dealers who still had large stocks on hand held cut-rate sales. A few actually dumped their stock rather than risk seizure.

In some nightclubs elaborate mock funerals were held. At the Golden Glades in New York City, a coffin was wheeled around the dance floor. At midnight everyone was encouraged to throw his or her last bottle or glass into it. Reisenweber's Cafe sent out black-bordered invitations to a "funeral ball." The band played Chopin's *Funeral March*. At the Hotel Vanderbilt's Della Robba Room, the tune was "Good-by Forever," and the management gave out the last of the champagne, free.

But in the nation's small towns and particularly in the churches, which had fought long and hard for Prohibition, the mood was joyful. In these places, there was genuine cause for celebration.

An invitation to a celebratory gathering at a Long Island, New York, Presbyterian church read:

> Let the church bells ring and let there be great rejoicing, for an enemy the equal of *Prussianism* [a word that meant German militarism] in frightfulness has been overthrown and victory crowns the efforts of the forces of righteousness. Let us see that no *Bolshevistic* [a word that meant Russian communism] liquor interests shall ever tear the Eighteenth Amendment from the Constitution of the United States.

And in Norfolk, Virginia, Billy Sunday, the ex-baseball player who had become America's most energetic and popular preacher, a man who had campaigned tirelessly against drinking, held a mock funeral for John Barleycorn, a popular name for liquor and the liquor industry.

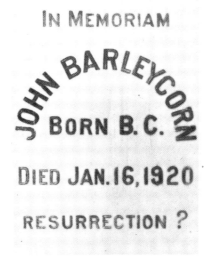

The citizens of Meriden, Connecticut, offered this tombstone in honor of their dear departed friend, "John Barleycorn."

A coffin containing a life-size rag doll representing John Barleycorn was carried through the streets by six black-clad pallbearers. A seventh man, wearing a devil costume—red tights, horns, and a tail—was the chief mourner. Inside the specially constructed hall, Sunday delivered a half-hour funeral oration, which had the overflow crowd convulsed with laughter.

But the funerals in New York and Norfolk were premature—for John Barleycorn proved to be a very lively corpse.

2

THE ALCOHOLIC REPUBLIC

The founders of the United States never envisioned anything like Prohibition. In its earliest days the nation seemed a most unlikely place to ban the drinking of alcoholic beverages. Later, those who objected to drinking were often labeled puritans. But the original Puritans, those who settled in New England, did not object to drinking. Though public drunkenness might be condemned and punished, drinking itself was not. In the late seventeenth century the Reverend Increase Mather, probably the most influential Puritan minister of his time, said that drink was "a good creature of God" and that man should partake of the gift without abusing it. He warned, however, that a man must not "drink a Cup of Wine more than is good for him."

His equally influential son, the Reverend Cotton Mather, was more concerned that drinking might pose a threat to established society. He encouraged people of the "Best Sort" to set a good example by not getting drunk.

Despite such warnings, throughout the American colonies men, women, and even children were downing stupendous quantities of highly potent hard cider and rum, without any restrictions and without guilt.

In 1744, Dr. Alexander Hamilton of Annapolis traveled throughout the colonies recording his observations. He said that the people of Philadelphia didn't seem to drink enough. In New York he found that heavy drinking was essential in good company. Governor George Clinton, "a jolly toaper" [toper, a word for drunkard] in Dr. Hamilton's view, matched him drink for drink. But the endless New York toasts were finally too much for Dr. Hamilton, who said he preferred to limit himself to a single bottle of wine each evening.

The amount of drinking that was done did begin to alarm some people, and they tried to set limits, not on the amount of drink consumed but on the number of taverns and public houses where the drinking took place. In 1760, John Adams asked the town meeting in Braintree, Massachusetts, to consider reducing the number of public houses. Adams was ridiculed and his proposal was overwhelmingly voted down.

John Adams probably drank the least of the Founding Fathers, but even he downed a tankard of hard cider with breakfast every morning. Hard cider has about twice the alcoholic content of beer. George Washington was, among other things, a whiskey distiller; Thomas Jefferson had one of the first vineyards in America, and customarily drank three glasses of wine a day.

In colonial America drinking was part of every private and public celebration. In 1758, when Washington campaigned for the House of Burgesses in Virginia, he worried that his election agent had not spent enough on liquor for the voters. He had lost an earlier election to a candidate who had provided drink more generously. Washington won in 1758 after giving out 144 gallons (545 liters) of rum, punch, wine, and hard cider. His vote total was 307, an investment of about half a gallon per vote.

The British claimed, with some justification, that the American Revolution was hatched in taverns. The common folk met in taverns to toast freedom, organize a militia, and plot their revolution. The pro-British Tory aristocrats, who did their drinking at home, condemned taverns as public nuisances and called all who went to them drunken enemies of the government.

The success of the Revolution resulted in a temporary increase in the prestige of the tavern and the collapse of any serious effort to control drinking. The greatest drinking holiday in the new republic was the Fourth of July.

In 1794 an attempt to enforce a tax on whiskey led to a serious revolt against the new American government in western Pennsylvania. Though the revolt, called the Whiskey Rebellion, was put down, it was a dramatic example of just how seriously many Americans took their whiskey as a source of revenue, and as a symbol of individual liberty.

There was no such thing as a minimum drinking age. American parents began trying to accustom their children to drinking practically from infancy, at least partly in the hope that this would protect them from becoming drunkards later on. "It is no uncommon thing," said one early nineteenth-century observer, "to see a boy of twelve or fourteen years old . . . walk into a tavern in the forenoon to take a glass of brandy and bitters."

There were many reasons for all the heavy drinking. Alcoholic spirits were easily available and cheap. Rum was made from sugarcane grown in the West Indies. During the Revolution, when trade with the West Indies was interrupted, Americans distilled home-grown grain into whiskey. Whiskey replaced rum as the drink of choice.

Often there was little else to drink. Water supplies were unreliable and sometimes dangerous. There were no soft drinks or bottled fruit juices. Without refrigeration, milk spoiled quickly. Tea was expensive and coffee even more expensive. Both had to be imported from distant lands.

The American diet, particularly on the frontier, was usually monotonous and extremely greasy. The flavor of whiskey helped overcome the monotony, and the alcohol cut the grease. Most people believed that alcohol was good for you, because it "kept up your strength."

Whiskey was a favorite trade item with Native Americans. For the Indians, whose entire culture was already under great stress, the introduction of liquor was a major disaster. Liquor was often used cynically, though effectively, by white traders and Indian agents to control Indians and their lands. They got the Indians drunk and cheated them. The tragic legacy of this policy is still evident, for alcoholism remains a major problem for Native Americans. Some of the first liquor laws passed in the United States were attempts to control the liquor trade to the Indians. These laws, however, were largely ineffective.

Dr. Rush Dissents

NOT EVERYONE IN AMERICA thought liquor was good for you. The most notable dissenter was Dr. Benjamin Rush, the best-known physician practicing in the United States. Rush was a friend of Benjamin Franklin and Thomas Paine, a member of the Second Continental Congress, a signer of the Declaration of Independence, and surgeon general of the Continental middle army during the Revolutionary War. In 1785 he published a paper entitled "Enquiry into the Effects of Spiritous Liquors upon the Human Body and Mind."

Dr. Rush had nothing against alcohol in general. He even suggested that moderate amounts of wine were good for health and helped people live longer. He thought that soldiers should be switched from hard liquor to malt drinks like beer. He considered opium far safer for the treatment of gastric disorders and mental depression than rum. The opium habit, the doctor said, was not hard to break. Dr. Rush was wrong, but this was a commonly held belief at the time.

He had almost nothing good to say about the effects of hard liquor. His paper was filled with horror stories about people whose lives had been ruined by rum and whiskey. A deeply religious man, Dr. Rush believed that Christianity was the best antidote for alcoholism. His "Enquiry" was reissued year after year, frequently quoted in the press, and widely distributed and discussed among the clergy. Dr. Rush has properly been called "the True Instaurator," that is, the one who started the antiliquor movement.

*Dr. Benjamin Rush, a respected physician and signer
of the Declaration of Independence, is credited with starting
the antiliquor movement in the United States.*

3

FROM TEMPERANCE TO TEETOTALISM

*B*y *the* 1840s, America's monumental post-Revolutionary drinking binge began to ease. People started drinking less—much less.

The reasons for the rapid and more or less permanent decline in heavy drinking among Americans are complex and, like most mass changes in behavior, are not really understood.

It's probable that the main reason for the change in drinking habits was the vast social changes that were taking place. The country had become more stable and more industrial. While there was still plenty of frontier, the majority of Americans no longer lived on it. They lived in cities, towns, and well-established farming communities. The rootlessness that so often led to heavy drinking was no longer as common.

Physicians, who had once prescribed alcohol as a remedy for practically everything, were taking a hard look at its dangers. And many began to adopt, at least in part, the program first set forth by Dr. Benjamin Rush.

*The Washingtonians were among the very first groups to produce a pledge
that they encouraged people to sign as their "Declaration of Independence" from
alcohol. The print was made in the mid-1800s to commemorate their efforts.*

Capitalists began to oppose drinking for very practical reasons.
In a slower-moving agrarian society drunkenness might be toler-
ated. If a trapper or sailor went out on an occasional "spree," that
did not interfere with his work. A drunken clerk, however, was of
little use. A worker in the mills and factories that were becoming
ever more important in America could not be drunk on the job

without slowing the entire operation, as well as risking injury or death to himself and others.

Long layoffs for a drinking bout and the necessary recovery time did not fit into the new more efficient system of work. The time spent in passing the jug around or standing round after round of drinks was no longer available to the worker. Heavy drinking meant waste and loss of profit. Drinking, which promised immediate gratification, conflicted with the new work ethic, which required delayed gratification or the gratification that came from hard work alone.

The tone of the growing antiliquor crusade was set by the Protestant churches. One of the most powerful voices was that of the Reverend Lyman Beecher, who some historians consider the true founder of the temperance, or antiliquor, movement. In 1826, Beecher delivered a series of six furious sermons in which liquor was denounced from every possible angle:

> Who can estimate the hatred of God, of his word and worship, and of his people which it [liquor] occasions. . . . How many thousands does it detain every Sabbath-day from the house of God—cutting them off from the means of grace . . . can we lawfully amass property [in the liquor trade] which fills the land with beggars and widows and crimes, which peoples graveyards with premature mortality, and the world of woe with victims of despair?

This was a long way from the Reverend Increase Mather's description of wine as "a good creature of God."

Lyman Beecher's daughter Harriet wrote tracts for the temperance movement, but her real fame came when she wrote the antislavery novel, *Uncle Tom's Cabin*. Before the Civil War many in

In later years, temperance pledges became elaborate documents, such as this one that features portraits of famous people who had "signed off."

the temperance movement were also strong supporters of the campaign to abolish slavery. Yet they often regarded drinking as worse than slavery. Slaves, they argued, had only lost control of their bodies, while drunkards had lost their souls. "The chains of intoxication," declared one enthusiastic reformer, "are heavier than those which the sons of Africa have ever worn."

In Lyman Beecher's day and for many years afterward the antiliquor movement was always called the temperance movement. The word "prohibition" was not used or even thought of at that time. But "temperance" is a misleading description, for it implies moderation in drinking alcohol. The early temperance societies did not demand that their members completely give up all alcohol. But within a few years tolerance for even moderate drinking completely disappeared. The pioneer American Temperance Society pledged new members to total abstinence, marking their names on the membership list with a T for "total." That is how the word "teetotaler," one who is opposed to all alcoholic drinks, came into the language. Though a variety of antiliquor organizations continued to use the word "temperance" in their name, they were in reality "teetotal" in outlook.

Women played an increasingly important role in the temperance movement. In 1874 a group called the Women's Crusade swept through Ohio. Their technique was to march in a group to a saloon or other place that sold liquor—and the more rowdy and notorious the place, the better. They would stand out front loudly singing and praying. Sometimes they actually entered the place to plead with the male drinkers to return to their families, and with the saloon keeper to cease his wicked trade. The women were ridiculed, doused with water, and sometimes even arrested, but they persisted with great vigor.

*An etching from a New York newspaper showing temperance
as very much of a women versus men issue.*

The Crusaders captured a lot of public attention, and a large number of saloons in Ohio and other parts of the Midwest actually did close down after a visit from the Crusaders. But their success was short-lived. Most of the saloon keepers who promised to "reform" reopened their establishments as soon as the excitement died down. When the Crusaders tried to spread out beyond their Midwestern base they ran into resistance. In the South even pro-temperance men denounced their activities as "unwomanly."

A far more successful organization was the Woman's Christian Temperance Union (WCTU). The WCTU was organized in 1874, and its success was due largely to the efforts of its extraordinary leader Frances Willard, an educator from Evanston, Illinois.

Frances Willard was a woman of boundless energy who possessed a genius for organization and persuasion. Her followers called her, without a hint of condescension, Saint Francis. In the twenty years that she ran the WCTU she made it into the largest all-woman organization in the world. One of her slogans was "Do everything"—and she did. She gave lectures all over the world, averaging about one a day. She wrote books and about twenty thousand letters a year. Her organization agitated and petitioned for many causes, from increasing the penalties for rape to improving education, but the basic issue for the WCTU was putting a stop to the liquor trade, making the sale and consumption of alcoholic beverages illegal.

When Frances Willard died in 1898 four states declared her birthday a holiday, and hundreds of schools, churches, community centers, hospitals, and parks were named after her. She was the first woman whose statue was placed in the Statuary Hall in the Capitol in Washington, D.C. She represents the state of Illinois.

This statue of Frances Willard, leader of the WCTU, stands in Statuary Hall of the U.S. Capitol Building.

"Smash, Smash, Smash!"

A TOUGH, BIG-BONED KANSAS woman named Carry Nation became the most visible symbol of the antiliquor crusade at the turn of the century. Until 1899, when she was fifty-three years old, Carry Nation was a fairly ordinary temperance worker and president of the local chapter of the WCTU. Then she decided that speeches and petitions were not enough. The sale of liquor was already prohibited by law in Kansas. But the law was widely ignored, and liquor was readily available in places called "joints." Mrs. Nation—sometimes with a few supporters, most often alone—marched into joints all over the state and quite literally broke them up. Her battle cry was "Smash, Smash. For the love of Jesus, Smash!" She was famous for using a hatchet to destroy places where liquor was sold, but she would also use a crow-

bar, a rock, or anything else that came to hand.

She moved her activities out of Kansas into areas where

the sale of liquor was not illegal. Carry Nation became a great favorite with reporters who followed her everywhere and recorded her activities in detail. The publicity made her famous. Some saloons hired extra guards when she was in town. Others actually welcomed her, figuring that the publicity was worth whatever damage she might do. Several saloons were named after her, and there was even a Carry Nation cocktail.

Nation was never really a leader of any movement, and more respectable antiliquor crusaders considered her an eccentric and something of an embarrassment. But everyone knew who Carry Nation was and what she stood for.

4

THE POLITICS OF PROHIBITION

The first temperance workers in the United States hoped and believed that people could be persuaded—or perhaps shamed—into abstinence. When that didn't work, they first campaigned to limit the sale of alcohol in various ways; and when that proved inadequate, to ban it entirely.

In 1851, Maine passed a strict general prohibition law. Before the law was passed, Maine had a reputation as one of the drunkest states in the nation. After the law was passed, its reputation did not change much. Over the next few years a dozen other states passed a variety of prohibitory laws. Statewide prohibition, however, proved to be extremely difficult and expensive to enforce. The laws just didn't work, and most were soon drastically modified or repealed entirely.

By then the nation was on the brink of civil war, and people had more immediate concerns. By the end of the war the once active temperance movement looked very nearly dead. In the

STEP 1.
A glass
with
a Friend.

STEP 2.
A glass to
keep the
cold out.

STEP 3.
A glass
too
much.

STEP 4.
Drunk
and
riotous.

STEP 5.
The summit attained
Jolly companions
A confirmed drunkard.

STEP 6.
Poverty
and
Disease.

STEP 7.
Forsaken
by
Friends.

STEP 8.
Desperation
and
crime.

STEP 9.
Death
by
suicide.

*Etchings such as this one depicting the progress of
the drunkard straight to his grave were designed to
shame or perhaps frighten people into abstinence.*

[29]

White House sat President Ulysses S. Grant who, despite a legendary love of whiskey, was elected, then reelected, by enormous majorities. In 1872, Grant crushed teetotaling Horace Greeley, nominee of both the Democratic and the Liberal Republican parties and James Black, nominee of the newly formed National Prohibition party.

Black polled a mere 5,607 votes. The Prohibition party's vote total grew steadily in subsequent elections, but it was never really an important factor in national elections. Far more important politically were the Protestant churches, organizations like the Woman's Christian Temperance Union (though women did not yet have the right to vote), and most specifically, the cunningly named Anti-Saloon League. The saloon, with its sawdust-covered floor, smell of stale beer, and general reputation for rowdiness, was the most notorious sort of drinking establishment in America. It was an easy target. But the League was not just against the saloon; it was against the drinking of any alcoholic beverages anywhere, ever.

The League was formed in Oberlin, Ohio, in 1893. It had strong ties to many Protestant churches, but not to any political party. The League kept track of elected officials from the local level to the Senate. It didn't make any difference which party an officeholder belonged to or how he voted on other issues. It didn't make any difference if he drank or even if he owned a saloon. If the officeholder voted "dry"—that is, in favor of what the League favored and against what it was against—the organization would support him. But if he did not vote the way the League wanted on every liquor issue, then the word went out to every church in his district, and the well-organized church members would vote him out. Among politicians the process was known as "getting hit on the head with a steeple."

A notable example of the League's power was displayed in the 1905 election for governor of Ohio. The Republican governor, Myron Herrick, was up for reelection. He had been a good governor, and was personally popular. The Democratic candidate was virtually unknown, and Ohio was usually an overwhelmingly Republican state. But Herrick had vetoed a bill the League had favored, which would have allowed localities to set strict rules about the sale of liquor. The League organized three thousand public meetings during the campaign, and distributed millions of pages of literature. Church members knocked on doors and rang doorbells. On election day Herrick lost by a landslide, and politicians all across the country got the message. The Anti-Saloon League could deliver the vote.

On the other side of the issue stood the United States Brewers' Association and the National Wholesale Liquor Dealers Association. Both associations were well financed and ready to spend whatever necessary to beat prohibition candidates and legislation. But all they had was money. They didn't have the volunteers to get out the votes on election day. They didn't have the moral high ground. The Anti-Saloon League could claim it was defending the family, God, morality in general. The brewers and liquor dealers looked as if all they were doing was defending their very profitable businesses. The methods used by the brewers and liquor dealers were heavy-handed, often amounting to little more than crude attempts to bribe politicians. They were continually running afoul of laws governing political campaigns and electioneering.

By using the saloon rather than drinking itself as the symbol of evil, the supporters of prohibition were using a powerful but often unspoken argument against liquor. The saloon was essentially an institution of cities. The fight over prohibition was in

*Women actually sat in saloons and kept written records of who purchased
how many drinks. Note the man setting loose a skunk in front of the stove,
a creative if not courageous way of driving the women from the bar!*

many respects a fight between the growing urban centers and the
still powerful small towns and rural areas. It was also a clash between native-born Protestant Americans and more recent—and often Catholic—Irish, Italian, and German immigrants who did not
consider drinking sinful.

When an organization of German Americans announced its op-
position to an antiliquor law, one prohibition periodical thundered,
"Really, is not the country growing rather tired of having a lot of

swill-fattened, blowsy half-foreigners getting together and between hiccoughs laying down definitions to Americans regarding the motive of our constitution and laws."

In the South, race often became part of the argument over liquor. Some evangelists argued that liquor "inflamed black rape fiends" and that prohibition would save "white womanhood" and reduce both the number of sex crimes and lynchings.

Appeals to prejudice, however, could work both ways, and one may actually have changed the outcome of a presidential election. The 1884 presidential election was shaping up as a close contest between the Republican nominee James G. Blaine and Democrat Grover Cleveland. Just a few days before the election Blaine made an appearance at a meeting of several hundred Protestant clergymen in New York City. One of the other speakers was the Reverend Samuel D. Burchard. Blaine sat on the platform smiling but perhaps not listening, as Burchard said: "We expect to vote for you next Tuesday. . . . We are Republicans, and don't propose to leave our party and identify ourselves with the party whose antecedents have been rum, Romanism, and rebellion."

Blaine did not react, but a Democrat in the audience did. By Sunday every Roman Catholic church in the state had a copy of Burchard's speech, with the three *r's* underlined. Blaine then loudly denied that he had condoned such a speech, but the election was two days away and it was too late.

The election was one of the closest in U.S. history. Cleveland won by 219 electoral votes to 182. If Blaine had carried New York State he would have won the election. He lost primarily because angry Catholic voters had turned against him.

But overall the political success of the antiliquor movement in America was impressive, particularly on the local and state levels.

By 1913, over half of the people in the United States lived under some form of prohibition. The piecemeal approach wasn't enough for organizations like the WCTU and the Anti-Saloon League. Local laws were too easy to get around—the only solution, they felt, was total nationwide prohibition.

In December 1913, five thousand drys (opponents of liquor) paraded from the White House to the Capitol. They carried banners calling for prohibition by 1920, the three-hundredth anniversary of the landing of the Pilgrims. They presented a petition to Congress asking for a constitutional amendment that would prohibit all alcoholic beverages. It was the first time such an action had been formally suggested.

Amending the U.S. Constitution isn't easy. It takes a two-thirds vote in each house of Congress, then ratification by the legislatures of three fourths of the states. The wets, who had been decisively outmaneuvered politically, still believed that national prohibition couldn't happen. Even the most optimistic of the drys figured on a tough uphill fight.

Then something happened that neither wets nor drys had foreseen: World War I broke out, and in 1917 the United States entered the war. The entire political climate of the nation changed. There was a massive outbreak of antiforeign sentiment, particularly anti-German. German Americans dominated the manufacture and sale of beer. Prohibition speakers often referred to "the un-American saloon." They also argued that grain and other ingredients of beer and hard liquor were needed for the war effort.

While most Americans were distracted by the war, leaders of the antiliquor movement had not lost their focus. They continued to press their elected representatives. The Eighteenth Amendment to the Constitution, which prohibited "the manufacture, sale or transportation of intoxicating liquors within, the importation thereof into, or the exportation thereof from the United States . . ." passed with little debate or excitement.

On August 1, 1917, the vote in the Senate, where rural districts held the balance of power, was 65 to 20. In the House, with a larger number of representatives from urban areas, the vote was closer, 282 to 128, on December 18.

Still, the opponents of Prohibition were confident that the necessary thirty-six states would not ratify, or approve, the Eighteenth Amendment within the seven-year time limit set by Congress. With a speed that astonished even the most ardent prohibitionists, the amendment was ratified in a mere thirteen months. In the end only two states, Connecticut and Rhode Island, refused to ratify. The Prohibition Amendment had been approved by a greater number, and a larger percentage, of the states than any of the previous seventeen amendments.

The wets argued that these votes were rammed through a war-weary nation by a determined minority and did not represent the will of the American people. That didn't make any difference. What had seemed impossible just a few years earlier had actually happened.

5

ENFORCING THE LAW

The Eighteenth Amendment was a mere three paragraphs long. The National Prohibition Act, which detailed what could and could not be done with alcoholic beverages and what the penalties were for those who broke the law, was a long, rambling document. It was commonly called the Volstead Act after Andrew Joseph Volstead, the Republican congressman from Minnesota who introduced the act in the House. The real author of the act, however, was Wayne Wheeler of the Anti-Saloon League.

The Volstead Act was finally adopted on October 10, 1919. President Woodrow Wilson thought it might be unconstitutional and vetoed it on October 28. Two hours later Congress overrode his veto, and the Volstead Act became law.

While the aim of the Volstead Act was very clearly to prevent people from consuming any beverage containing more than one-half of one percent of alcohol, there were all sorts of loopholes, or exceptions. For example, a farmer could make cider—then store it and let it "harden," that is, become alcoholic. So long as he didn't add anything to it, or treat it in any way, and didn't try to sell it, the beverage was perfectly legal. This was a concession to the politically powerful farmers.

Beer could still be brewed legally. But before it could be sold, almost all of the alcohol had to be removed. The end product was something popularly called "near beer." It wasn't "near" enough for the beer-drinking public. So before being sold the beer was often sprayed with alcohol from a hypodermic needle to bring it up to its old-time strength. That was illegal, but "needle beer" became a staple of the Prohibition Era. And the alcohol drawn off the legally produced beer was frequently sold to make other illegal beverages.

Another popular and perfectly legal product was grape concentrate. A brick of the concentrate was dissolved in a gallon of water. Then the user was warned, "Do not place the liquid in this jug and put it away in the cupboard for twenty-one days, because then it would turn into wine." During Prohibition the sale of grapes and all the paraphernalia needed for making wine at home increased dramatically. The vineyards of California, where grapes are grown for wine, prospered.

It wasn't legal to distill alcohol at home. But it was easy. Even before Prohibition, making "home brew," or "moonshine" as it was often called, was common, particularly in the rural South. With the start of Prohibition the practice spread to the cities. The equipment cost only a few dollars, and instructions could be found in bulletins published by the government, between 1906 and 1910, explaining how to distill alcohol from grain, sugar beets, and potato peelings. One product was known as "bathtub gin" because when water was added, it required a container too large to fit in an ordinary kitchen sink, so it was put under the tap in the bathtub.

Liquor was still legally available for medicinal purposes through pharmacies. Some unscrupulous pharmacists would get phony prescriptions from equally unscrupulous doctors or simply forge them. Then they would go to the government warehouses and get the liquor the prescriptions entitled them to. The liquor would be "cut," that is, mixed with other substances, so the pharmacist now had three or four bottles instead of one.

The easiest way to get around the Volstead Act was to be in the industrial alcohol business. Alcohol was needed in the manufacture of a huge number of products from paint to toothpaste. The business could not be shut down, and during the Prohibition Era the production of industrial alcohol increased dramatically. Much of it—no one knows how much—went into the manufacture of illegal beverages.

When it came out of the factory industrial alcohol was poisonous. But it could be "washed," that is, the poisons could be removed. Sometimes they were, sometimes they were not, and many people died or went blind from drinking liquor made from industrial alcohol.

Prohibition agents proudly display their "take" in Washington, D.C., where, in 1922, they claimed to have shut down the largest still in the city.

A cartoon poking fun at the loopholes in the Volstead Act.
It was captioned "The Drug Store of the Future" and shows
people enthusiastically lined up for "medicinal" liquors.

As the Prohibition Era opened, leaders of the antiliquor movement sincerely believed that the Volstead Act could be enforced easily and cheaply. Wayne Wheeler estimated that enforcement would cost about five million dollars a year. Like other die-hard drys, he was convinced that the American public would soon recognize the enormous value of an alcohol-free society, and the need for enforcement would rapidly disappear. It was the greatest miscalculation he ever made.

Congress appropriated $6,350,000 for the first year of enforcement. By 1923, the secretary of the treasury asked for $28,500,000 for enforcement, and a few years later it was estimated that at least $300,000,000 would be needed.

Both the Eighteenth Amendment and the Volstead Act allowed states to pass their own prohibition laws. Many did, and some laws were a lot tougher than the federal statutes. In Vermont, for example, people arrested for drunkenness were required to tell the authorities who had given or sold them the liquor.

The trouble was that the states appropriated even less money for enforcement than the federal government. The general attitude seemed to be that Prohibition was a federal problem. The states also soon discovered that if they made arrests under their own laws, the cases would have to be tried in state courts and that was time-consuming and expensive. Besides, a large percentage of the cases were dismissed, or the defendants if found guilty were given trifling sentences. As a result, states usually didn't enforce their own laws and were uncooperative with federal authorities.

The leaders of the Prohibition movement had assumed that as people got used to the idea they would increasingly respect the

Izzy & Moe

THE FRONT LINE IN THE WAR against illegal alcohol were the agents of the Prohibition Unit (later called Prohibition Bureau). There were about 1,500 of them. They were poorly paid, barely trained, often corrupt, and widely despised. There weren't enough agents to make a serious dent in the liquor trade. It was expected that they would cooperate with local law enforcement, but such cooperation was rare.

The most successful and certainly the most colorful of the Prohibition agents were Isidor Einstein and his friend Moe Smith—known to newspaper readers throughout America as Izzy and Moe. Izzy had been a postal clerk, Moe the owner of a small cigar store. Using an astonishing number of strategies and disguises, they were able to arrest almost 5,000 suspects in their five-year career. To gain entrance to places where liquor was sold they impersonated tourists, farmers, and street cleaners, wealthy playboys, out-of-work actors, and gravediggers. Izzy once even impersonated himself, when he told a bartender, "I'm Izzy Einstein—the Prohibition agent." The bartender laughed, served him a drink, and was arrested!

Izzy and Moe loved publicity. They often invited the press along when they made an arrest. Izzy was about five feet tall and weighed over two hundred and fifty pounds. His picture was in the newspapers so many times it is a wonder that he was able to fool anyone.

Izzy and Moe were too successful and too popular. Their superiors became jealous. In November 1925 both men were fired. A Prohibition Bureau spokesman said: "The service must be dignified. Izzy and Moe belong on the vaudeville stage."

Izzy and Moe undercover

law. Just the opposite happened. The law was increasingly ignored by people in all walks of life.

Prohibition-era President Warren G. Harding had been a senator from Ohio, one of the states where antiliquor sentiment ran most strongly. While in Congress, Harding had helped push through the Eighteenth Amendment. But he was an easygoing, whiskey-loving man. When he was in the White House he and his cronies from back home, called the Ohio Gang, gathered twice a week for a session of poker and drinking. The whiskey was supplied by the treasurer of the Republican National Committee.

Congressman M. Alfred Michaelson of Illinois was such an enthusiastic dry that he had wanted harsher penalties than those imposed by the Volstead Act. In January 1928 he returned from a West Indian cruise. One of his trunks sprang a leak, and it was found to contain thirteen bottles of whiskey. Another held a ten-gallon keg of rum. Michaelson's brother-in-law swore the trunks belonged to him and was fined $1,000.

In New York City there was a popular little rhyme that ran:

> *Mother's in the kitchen*
> *Washing out the jugs;*
> *Sister's in the pantry*
> *Bottling the suds;*
> *Father's in the cellar*
> *Mixing up the hops;*
> *Johnny's on the front porch*
> *Watching for the cops.*

6

BOOTLEGGERS AND RUM RUNNERS

Before Prohibition most Americans were essentially law-abiding people. But Prohibition turned many into lawbreakers. People just didn't think that there was anything wrong with having a few drinks. Besides, it seemed as if everyone was doing it. While some people fermented their own wine and distilled their own alcohol, most people bought their liquor from a bootlegger or at places generally called speakeasies. Both words predate Prohibition. "Bootlegger" was a term used for men who sold illegal liquor to the Indians; they often concealed bottles in the tops of their boots. "Speakeasy" comes from Ireland, where drinks were sold illegally in "speak softly shops." Prohibition made the words a familiar part of the American language.

To most people the local bootlegger or neighborhood bartender was someone who supplied a needed service, and not a "real" criminal. But those who supplied the bootleggers and the bartenders with the liquor *were* "real" criminals by anybody's definition. And since the illegal liquor was one of the biggest businesses in the country, they became increasingly rich and powerful criminals.

The first large-scale organized criminal activity of the Prohibition Era was smuggling. The United States was trying to be a dry island in a wet world. The manufacture, importation, and sale of alcoholic beverages was perfectly legal in Canada, Mexico, and the Caribbean. The United States has a lot of seacoast and long, poorly guarded borders.

As soon as Prohibition went into effect there was a dramatic increase in Mexican imports of scotch whiskey from Britain. The Mexicans weren't drinking more; eventually all of this whiskey made its way north across the border.

Canada had manufactured a small amount of whiskey before Prohibition. After Prohibition it became a major manufacturer, and its imports from Britain also took a jump. This liquor made its way south by truck or by boat across the Great Lakes. The United States tried to get Canada to exercise tighter controls on the liquor trade. But it was so profitable that Canadian authorities dragged their feet for years.

The most spectacular smugglers were the rum runners, though they brought in more scotch than rum. The rum runners operated small boats that were often fitted with false bottoms and secret compartments. They picked up their cargo in the Caribbean and unloaded it on Long Island, the beaches of New Jersey, near Boston—practically anywhere on the East Coast. Later a second "rum row" opened up on the West Coast. Here the cargoes came from Mexico or Western Canada.

All of this took money—to buy the trucks and boats, to bribe customs officials and police. And it took violence—a willingness to shoot it out with the Coast Guard, the police, and rival gangs who tried to steal the liquor.

Hijacking was another way of getting the liquor. Early in the Prohibition Era there was still a lot of liquor locked away in government warehouses to be sold for medicinal purposes. Much of this was simply stolen by the criminals, particularly while it was being transported.

As time went on the criminals found it was even more profitable to manufacture their own liquor and beer. In Pittsburgh beer lovers paid a premium price for a brew they thought was being smuggled in from Canada. It turned out that a Pittsburgh gang was operating its own brewery in an abandoned slaughterhouse. The gangsters also printed counterfeit Canadian labels and pasted them on the bottles. They charged premium prices without the trouble and expense of trucking the stuff all the way down from Canada.

Distilling scotch or other liquors is a long and difficult process. It is quicker, easier, and far more profitable to simply distill pure grain alcohol—a product often called "white lightning." During Prohibition the alcohol was sold in two ways. It went straight from the distillery to the taverns in tin cans, or it was bottled with other ingredients and colorings that made it look and taste at least a little like real scotch, gin, or brandy. In other operations poisonous industrial alcohol was "washed," or turned into a drinkable and highly potent product.

Gangster-controlled liquor was sold everywhere. There were the "shock houses" on the New York streets called the Bowery that made even the worst of the old-time saloons look good. Here raw, or often deadly, alcohol was sold to the desperate. In 1928 alone over 700 people on the Bowery died from drinking it. At the other end of the social scale was the El Fay Club on West Forty-

*The Washington, D.C. police chase bootleggers in a car
equipped with a smoke screen device.*

fifth Street. It was owned by mobster Larry Fay, but the manager and best-known figure was May Louise "Texas" Guinan, a former circus bronco rider. As customers entered she would bellow her greeting, "Hello, sucker!" It became the catchphrase of the Prohibition Era.

Despite the optimistic predictions of the drys, America's taste for alcohol seemed to be growing rather than shrinking. And the profits being made from this trade were enormous—and, of course, tax free. Various gangs carried out vicious and bloody wars with one another over control of the liquor trade in a particular area. The most successful gangs became ever larger and more organized. With the money made from liquor they were able to branch out into a variety of other criminal enterprises, and eventually they used the money to take over legitimate businesses. The structure of what we now call organized crime was born during Prohibition.

The smuggling, rum running, and hijacking; the illegal distilleries and breweries; the speakeasies and the bootleggers; even the growing number of gangland murders could not have taken place without a lot of cooperation from the politicians and the police. In many cities and towns bribery had become a way of life. The huge profits made from the illegal liquor trade were corrupting American society. And everybody who bought a drink—and that may have included the majority of Americans—was contributing to the corruption.

A Ben Shahn painting showing federal
agents dumping wine down the sewer.

The Celebrity Gangster

ALPHONSE "AL" CAPONE, THE criminal boss of Chicago during Prohibition, was more famous than the mayor, the senators, perhaps even the president. Capone started his career as a bouncer in a New York nightclub. He became the protégé of John Torrio, who worked for his uncle, Chicago mobster Big Jim Colosimo. Torrio knew that Prohibition would offer enormous opportunities for the enterprising criminal. But Big Jim wasn't interested. Less than four months after Prohibition went into effect Colosimo was shot to death. Torrio and Capone were suspected, but nothing was ever proved.

Torrio and Capone immediately began to organize their bootlegging activities. Torrio proposed that the city be divided up into territories, each under the control of a specific gang, and that there would be no attempts to muscle in on anybody else's area. That plan never really worked very well. Disputes arose that were usually settled with gunfire.

In 1925, after Torrio was nearly killed by a rival gang, he retired and left the entire criminal enterprise in the hands of the more violent Capone. The most notorious act of Capone violence took place on February 14, 1929, Valentine's Day. Capone henchmen, some dressed as policemen, caught members of a rival gang in a warehouse on North Clark Street, where they were supposed to be picking up a hijacked truckload of whiskey. Seven men were lined up against the wall and machine-gunned. This became known as the Saint Valentine's Day Massacre.

Occasionally Capone tried to improve his public image.

After giving food and clothing to the poor, he told newspaper reporters: "I'll bet I've given a million dollars. I'm just saying this to show I'm not the worst man in the world."

Though he committed a huge number of crimes, including multiple murders, Al Capone could never be convicted of anything in Chicago. He was too powerful. Finally, federal authorities got him for income tax evasion. In 1931 he was sentenced to eleven years in jail. He spent most of his time in Alcatraz, the toughest prison in the country. Capone was released in 1939 when his health failed, and he died on his estate in Florida in 1947.

Al Capone winks at photographers as he leaves the court in Chicago. He was being tried on income tax evasion, a crime for which he was jailed for eight years.

7

THE NOBLE EXPERIMENT ENDS

In 1928, Republican presidential candidate Herbert Hoover called Prohibition a "Noble Experiment." But by that time it was clear that the experiment was failing. Even the Prohibition leaders were no longer predicting that a happy, alcohol-free America was just around the corner. The best they could do was ask for stricter enforcement, tougher penalties. They wanted industrial alcohol to be made even more poisonous, so that it would be more difficult to convert into a drinkable liquid. Wayne Wheeler of the Anti-Saloon League said, "The person who drinks this industrial alcohol is a deliberate suicide." Opponents said that the government was trying to enforce the law by deliberately poisoning violators.

The Nineteenth Amendment, granting women the right to vote, had been ratified just seven months after the Eighteenth Amendment. The drys had assumed this would make Prohibition repeal-proof. Men might be divided on the issue, but women, who had once been the leaders of the temperance movement, were thought to be solidly antiliquor. That was another miscalculation. Before Prohibition, respectable women never went into a saloon. But perfectly respectable women were going to speakeasies and dealing with bootleggers. And some became leaders in the growing movement calling for repeal of the Eighteenth Amendment.

Still, the drys possessed enormous political power, and it didn't seem as if repeal was something that could be accomplished quickly, if at all. But Prohibition was overtaken by events.

It was said that if there had been no World War I there would have been no Prohibition, and if there had been no Great Depression there would have been no Repeal. That's probably an exaggeration, but there is no doubt that these two calamitous events did influence Americans' attitudes toward liquor.

In 1929 the Stock Market crashed, and by 1930 businesses were failing and great numbers of people were being thrown out of work. Soon one out of four workers was unemployed. The Great Depression had begun. Government revenues fell as well. People began to look back with nostalgia to the days when the government collected great sums in taxes on liquor. Prohibition had ended that. People were drinking as much as ever, perhaps more, but all the money was going into the pockets of the gangsters. The government was actually spending money trying to enforce unenforceable laws.

Businessmen who had once been among the most influential supporters of Prohibition began to switch sides. So did their wives. In May 1929, Mrs. Charles H. Sabin, wife of a prominent banker and the first woman member of the Republican National Committee, became president of the Women's Organization for National Prohibition Reform. The organization was a smashing success from the start. In less than two years it had almost a million and a half members. They were sending speakers all over the country, even into some churches. Prohibitionists denounced them as "scarlet women," but accusations like that weren't being taken seriously anymore.

The opponents of Prohibition were no longer just a bunch of greedy brewers and liquor dealers with foreign-sounding names. They were some of the most respectable and respected people in the country.

Public opinion polling was still at a primitive stage in the early 1930s, but newspaper and magazine surveys indicated that an ever-increasing majority of men and women favored either modification or outright repeal of Prohibition. This was not lost on the politicians. By the 1932 presidential election Prohibition wasn't even an issue. It was doomed no matter who won.

Democrat Franklin Delano Roosevelt had waffled on the issue for years, but he came down firmly for Repeal when he accepted the nomination of his party. Republican President Herbert Hoover, who had really tried to enforce Prohibition during his term, switched sides before the 1932 election and said that control of liquor should be given back to the states. That enraged the drys who had supported him, and gained him few votes from the wets who generally favored Roosevelt and the Democrats. Roosevelt won in a landslide, but it was the Depression, not Prohibition, that dominated the election.

On December 6, 1932, just a month after Roosevelt's election, a congressional resolution was drafted calling for submission to the states of the Twenty-First Amendment, which would repeal the Eighteenth. Two months later both houses adopted it. Even before the states ratified the Repeal Amendment, President Roosevelt asked Congress to modify the Volstead Act to the extent of legalizing real beer.

The prohibitionists were not the only impassioned group. Those who wanted to end Prohibition launched equally lively counterattacks.

Billy Sunday, who had once pronounced a funeral oration for John Barleycorn, thundered: "Somebody should smash the noses of our Congressmen! It's an insult to America! We don't want beer!" He was wrong. It took only nine days for Congress to go along with the President's request. On the first day that beer was made legal a million and a half barrels were consumed, resulting in a nationwide shortage.

The procedure by which states ratified this constitutional amendment was different and more complicated than that used to ratify the Eighteenth and other amendments. Each state was to hold a referendum and, if Repeal won, to summon a convention whose delegates would cast their final ballots in favor of the amendment. It was expected that the process would take years. But the states moved with such speed that by December 1933 the necessary thirty-six states had ratified the Twenty-First Amendment, repealing Prohibition.

On December 5, 1933, President Roosevelt signed the proclamation ending Prohibition. The Noble Experiment had lasted thirteen years, ten months, and eighteen days.

After Repeal a few states chose to remain dry. But by 1966 there was not a single dry state left in the nation. State and local governments do regulate where and when liquor can be sold, and these regulations differ a great deal from place to place. During the 1960s and 1970s there was a move among the states to lower the age at which one could legally buy alcoholic beverages from twenty-one to eighteen years. But by the 1980s growing concerns over teenage drinking and driving reversed the trend, and the twenty-one-year-old drinking age is now virtually universal in the United States.

The end of Prohibition is celebrated as the first truckload of beer exits the Jacob Ruppert's Brewery in New York City.

Further Reading

Allen, Frederick Lewis. *Only Yesterday: An Informal History of the Nineteen Twenties*. New York: Harper, 1931.

Chidsey, Donald Barr. *On and Off the Wagon*. New York: Cowles Book Co., 1969.

Cohen, Susan and Daniel. *A Six Pack and a Fake I.D.* New York: M. Evans and Co., 1986.

Kobler, John. *Ardent Spirits: The Rise and Fall of Prohibition*. New York: Putnam, 1973.

Waller, Leslie. *The Mob: The Story of Organized Crime in America*. New York: Delacorte, 1973.

Bibliography

Algren, Nelson. *Chicago: City on the Make*. New York: Doubleday, 1951.

Allsop, Kenneth. *The Bootleggers: The Story of Chicago's Prohibition Era*. New Rochelle, NY: Arlington House, 1968.

Asbury, Herbert. *Carry Nation: The Woman With the Hatchet*. New York: Knopf, 1929.

Binger, Carl. *Revolutionary Doctor: Benjamin Rush*. New York: Norton, 1966.

Dobyns, Fletcher. *The Amazing Story of Repeal*. Chicago: Willett Clark and Co., 1940.

Earhart, Mary. *Frances Willard: From Prayer to Politics*. Chicago: University of Chicago Press, 1944.

Furnas, J. C. *The Late Demon Rum*. New York: Putnam, 1965.

Kobler, John. *Capone.* New York: Putnam, 1971.

Lee, Henry. *How Dry We Were.* Englewood Cliffs, NJ: Prentice-Hall, 1963.

McLoughlin, William G., Jr. *Billy Sunday Was His Real Name.* Chicago: University of Chicago Press, 1955.

Rorabaugh. W. J. *The Alcoholic Republic: An American Tradition.* New York: Oxford University Press, 1979.

Sinclair, Andrew. *Prohibition: The Era of Excess.* Boston: Little, Brown, 1962.

Walker, Stanley. *The Night Club Era.* New York: Frederick A. Stokes, 1933.

Chronology

1785	Dr. Benjamin Rush publishes "Enquiry into the Effects of Spiritous Liquors upon the Human Body and Mind."
1826	Reverend Lyman Beecher delivers six sermons against drinking.
1840	The Washingtonians, America's first temperance society, is formed.
1851	Maine passes the first statewide prohibition law.
1861	The Civil War begins.
1872	The Prohibition party nominates James Black as its first presidential candidate.
1873	The Woman's Christian Temperance Union (WCTU) is organized.

1893   The Anti-Saloon League is organized.

1913   December: Thousands of "drys" march on Washington de-
            manding a Prohibition Amendment to the Constitution.

1917   April 6: The United States enters World War I.

            December 18: Congress passes the Eighteenth, or Prohibi-
            tion, Amendment.

1919   January 16: The Eighteenth Amendment is ratified by the
            states.

            October 28: The National Prohibition Act (Volstead Act)
            is passed.

1920   January 16: Prohibition begins.

1929   February 14: St. Valentine Day's Massacre.

            May: Women's Organization for National Prohibition Reform
            is organized.

            October 29: Stock Market crashes.

1932   December 6: The Twenty-First, or Repeal, Amendment is
            introduced in Congress. It passes in two months.

1933   December 5: Prohibition ends.

Index